The Little Sewing and Weaving

by Sally Featherstone

Illustrations by Marion Lindsay

LITTLE BOOKS WITH BIG IDEAS

Published 2009 by A&C Black Publishers Limited
36 Soho Square, London W1D 3QY
www.acblack.com

ISBN 978-1-4081-1247-2

Text © Sally Featherstone
Illustrations © Marion Lindsay

With thanks to Sam Goodman for the main cover photograph.

A CIP record for this publication is available from the British Library.

Printed in Great Britain by Latimer Trend & Company Limited.

This book is produced using paper that is made from wood grown in
managed, sustainable forests. It is natural, renewable and recyclable.

The logging and manufacturing processes conform to the environmental
regulations of the country of origin.

**To see our full range of titles
visit www.acblack.com**

Contents

Introduction

The Early Years Foundation Stage (EYFS) guidance emphasises the importance of skills development through enjoyable and motivating activities. In particular, it stresses how vital fine motor skills are for future learning and success, both in school and in life. Crafts and creativity are at the heart of the Early Years' curriculum: the colour and vitality of children's work should be evident in every setting, where it is valued, discussed and displayed with respect and professionalism.

The Little Book of Sewing and Weaving builds on your creative work with the children by focusing on working with fabrics – sewing, stitching, weaving, constructing, wrapping, threading and much more. The activities are all adaptable for children of different ages and stages of development, and every one will help the children to develop their skills of fine motor control and hand/eye coordination.

Some of these activities will be familiar to you, some will be new, and some will be those that you have used in the past and that reappear as a new version or as a reminder of activities you enjoyed at home or in school when you were a child. The ideas become more challenging as you work through the book, but all the activities are suitable for children in Nursery and Reception groups. Some are appropriate for younger children to do, with significant adult support, or to watch and enjoy the process and the product.

Each activity follows the same format, with simple instructions for:

▶ What you need
▶ What you do
▶ Extensions and further activities (And another idea...)
▶ Links with the EYFS goals, so you can be sure that
  children are working towards relevant skills and knowledge.

Of course, you will want to give children plenty of practice in free play with fabrics, glue, fixings, string etc. before, around and after adult-initiated activities described in the book, and children will often want to return to an activity they have done with you by including it in their child-initiated play. Teach the children how to use and take care of the tools and equipment provided, and then you will be able to leave an activity you have done with a small group for further free exploration with minimum adult supervision. Some of the best experiences follow skilled adult support, when children revisit the activities in their own play.

The following features of learning are all important in gaining and practising sewing and fabric skills, but please note – they are not presented here in any order of priority!

▶ Exploring and talking about new resources, materials and fabrics

▶ Introducing new tools and teaching children how to use them

▶ Talking about creativity, making things and planning for making your own creations

▶ Watching and listening to people who are creative or have creative hobbies – parents, artists and craftspeople, visiting exhibitions, museums and galleries, and looking at the work of older children

▶ Looking at examples of creativity in books and pictures, and on the Internet

▶ Free play with new resources and equipment

▶ Talking about how to do things, concentrating, doing difficult things and about sometimes needing help

▶ Adult modelling of skills and activities so children can see how they are done, but without implying that the children will be able to perfect the skill immediately, or that there is only one right way of doing things

▶ Getting things out and putting them away safely and tidily

▶ Helping children to acquire new skills by giving physical and verbal support for the process

▶ Recognising children's achievements in words and expressions, and by displaying, photographing and using the things the children create

▶ Encouraging independence and creative thinking by noticing when children take an idea further or in a different direction

▶ Joining children in their child-chosen activities without making judgements or taking over

▶ Giving children opportunities to contribute to the setting and their families by making objects and small gifts that are either decorative or useful (or even both).

Collecting, preparing and storing your resources

Whether you are considering including sewing in your planning as a new area of activity, or want to extend what you do already, we are including here some ideas for the sorts of resources you may want to collect in your sewing cupboard and ways you can store them (see also page 80).

Storage

You may want to make a special place for sewing and fabric equipment and tools. This doesn't exclude the children from accessing them, but makes them aware that special tools are used for special activities. Of course, free access to sequins, buttons, shiny fabric and other special items may not be possible for financial and organisational reasons!

You may decide to use one or more of these ideas for storing your sewing and fabric stuff:

▶ a sewing box or basket – a small toolbox or hobby box with compartments, or a basket with a fabric lining to hold scissors, needles and essential specialist equipment;

▶ transparent plastic hobby boxes for the collection of buttons, beads, laces, strings and other small items;

▶ needle boxes with pictorial labels or pincushions for needles, mapping pins and safety pins;

▶ a vegetable rack with recycled materials, such as polystyrene wiggles, carrier bags, strips of fabric, pieces of felt, glue in dispensers etc. organised in separate baskets;

▶ plastic baskets on open shelves, with sorted fabrics and a piece of the fabric stuck on the end of the basket for a label;

▶ small sewing sets for individuals and pairs of children, stored in little baskets or buckets, so they are easy to handle. They could contain a couple of pairs of scissors, needles and other essentials for free play indoors or outside. Make a pictorial label so the children can check the contents when they have finished working;

▶ sewing cushions, beanbags, chairs or small mats where children can sit and sew in quiet areas of your setting.

Make sewing a permanent feature in your setting, so the children go to it as naturally as they select materials for painting, construction, malleable materials or books.

Implements and tools

It is very important to have effective tools and equipment for children to use in fabric work. Cutting or sewing with blunt or inappropriate tools will lead to frustration for you and for them. Children's tools must be fit for purpose, and you may decide to use small versions of adult tools to supplement those made specifically for children. You will also need some adult tools, so you can prepare and model the skills you are expecting the children to acquire.

A sewing box or basket should include the following tools:

Essential	Desirable	Specialist
▶ sharp, round-ended children's scissors ▶ adult scissors (keep a pair especially for fabric, so they stay sharp) ▶ children's needles (plastic and metal) ▶ adult needles in several sizes	▶ small-sized adult scissors (Fiskars make classic sewing scissors) ▶ scissors with patterned blades ▶ pinking shears ▶ needle threaders ▶ hole punch	▶ left-handed and 'teaching' scissors (see 'Resources and contacts' on page 80)

Make sure you check all your tools regularly, to ensure they are still sharp and working well. Watch the children as they work, and if they are having difficulty or getting frustrated, make sure they have the tools they need.

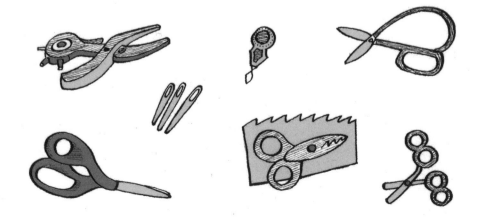

Standard resources

A sewing box or cupboard should include the following resources:

Essential

- sticky-backed plastic
- masking tape
- duct tape
- PVA glue in large quantities
- food colouring
- cold water dyes
- Brusho
- laces, strings and cord
- beads of all types
- sequins of all sizes and shapes
- glitter
- buttons
- fake jewels
- pipe cleaners

- small sticky scraps, flowers and other craft items
- pipe cleaners
- 'googly' eyes
- fabric crayons and fabric paints
- Binca and canvas
- plastic canvases
- felt in a range of colours
- ribbon
- braid
- trimmings
- tape
- string
- wool
- elastic

- plastic bin liners
- display folders with plastic covers and sleeves in A4 and A3 sizes to display individual work, creations and photos
- green garden sticks and canes
- digital camera
- plastic-coated garden netting

Recycled and reused materials

Essential

- leaves, twigs and other natural materials
- plastic carriers
- vegetable and fruit nets
- card
- old and broken crayons
- plastic trays from fruit and vegetables
- the spare buttons you get with clothes
- polystyrene packaging and packing pieces

- foam
- old picture frames and mirrors
- wooden and strong card boxes and crates
- sticks and twigs
- clean, unwanted tights, socks, gloves and mittens
- sheets
- clean shirts and other clothes
- net curtains
- bubble wrap
- plastic bags

Some suggested fabrics for your store cupboard

Desirable	
▶ brocade	▶ open weave
▶ chiffon	▶ plastic
▶ cord	▶ sari satin
▶ cotton	▶ seersucker
▶ crimplene	▶ silk
▶ denim	▶ suede and leather
▶ foils and shiny fabrics	▶ tee shirt
▶ fleece	▶ towelling
▶ fur fabric	▶ tweed
▶ jersey	▶ velvet
▶ knitted fabrics	▶ Velcro
▶ lace	▶ vilene
▶ Lycra	▶ voile
▶ net	

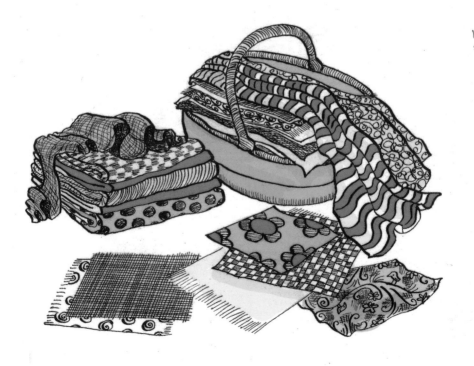

Early Learning Goals

The following goals are relevant to the activities in this book. They naturally include **Creative Development** and **Knowledge and Understanding of the World**, but we must also recognise the contribution that creative activities make to **Communication, Language and Literacy**, and particularly to **Personal, Social and Emotional Development**.

Personal, Social and Emotional Development

Dispositions and attitudes

▶ Shows an interest in classroom activities through observation or participation.

▶ Displays high levels of involvement in self-chosen activities.

▶ Selects and uses activities and resources independently.

▶ Continues to be interested, motivated and excited to learn.

▶ Is confident to try new activities, initiate ideas and speak in a familiar group.

▶ Maintains attention and concentrates.

▶ Sustains involvement and perseveres, particularly when trying to solve a problem or reach a satisfactory conclusion.

Social development

▶ Works as part of a group or class, taking turns and sharing fairly.

▶ Takes into account the ideas of others.

Emotional development

▶ Responds to significant experiences, showing a range of feelings when appropriate.

Communication, Language and Literacy

Language for communication and thinking

▶ Listens and responds.

▶ Talks activities through, reflecting on and modifying actions.

▶ Interacts with others in a variety of contexts, negotiating plans and activities, and taking turns in conversation.

▶ Speaks clearly with confidence and control, showing awareness of the listener.

▶ Talks and listens confidently and with control, consistently showing awareness of the listener by including relevant detail.

▶ Uses language to work out and clarify ideas, showing control of a range of appropriate vocabulary.

Reading

▶ Shows an understanding of how information can be found in non-fiction texts to answer questions about where, who, why and how.

Writing

▶ Attempts writing for a variety of purposes, using features of different forms.

Problem Solving, Reasoning and Numeracy

Calculating

▶ Uses developing mathematical ideas and methods to solve practical problems.

Shape, space and measures

▶ Describes shapes in simple models, pictures and patterns.

▶ Talks about, recognises and recreates simple patterns.

▶ Uses everyday words to describe position.

▶ Uses language such as 'circle' or 'bigger' to describe the shape and size of solids and flat shapes.

Knowledge and Understanding of the World

▶ Shows curiosity and interest by exploring surroundings.

▶ Observes, selects and manipulates objects and materials.

▶ Investigates objects and materials by using all their senses as appropriate.

▶ Looks closely at similarities, differences, patterns and change.

▶ Finds out about past and present events in their own life, and in those of family members and other people they know. Begins to know about their own culture and beliefs, and those of other people.

▶ Builds and constructs with a wide range of objects, selecting appropriate resources, tools and techniques and adapting their work where necessary.

Physical Development

▶ Constructs in a purposeful way, using simple tools and techniques.

▶ Demonstrates fine motor control and coordination.

▶ Uses small and large equipment, showing a range of basic skills.

▶ Handles tools, objects, construction and malleable materials safely and with basic control.

▶ Demonstrates coordination and control in large and small movements, and in using tools and equipment

Creative Development

▶ Explores different media and responds to a variety of sensory experiences.

▶ Tries to capture experiences, using a variety of different media.

▶ Explores colour, texture, shape, form and space in two or three dimensions.

▶ Uses imagination in art and design. Responds in a variety of ways to what they see, hear, smell, touch and feel.

▶ Expresses and communicates ideas, thoughts and feelings using a range of materials, suitable tools, imaginative role play, movement, designing and making, and a variety of songs and musical instruments.

▶ Expresses feelings and preferences in response to artwork, drama and music, and makes some comparisons and links between different pieces. Responds to their own work and that of others when exploring and communicating ideas, feelings and preferences through art.

NOTE

On each activity page, we have concentrated on significant goals for two or three areas of learning.

The
Activities

Threading – on a string

Threading through holes is a key skill in preparing for sewing, so give plenty of practice in making decorations, strings and necklaces with natural or bought objects.

What you need

- ▶ wool, soft string or laces
- ▶ anything with holes
  - ▷ buttons
  - ▷ pasta tubes or other shapes
  - ▷ beads
  - ▷ washers (metal, felt or card) and nuts
  - ▷ curtain rings
  - ▷ ring pulls from cans

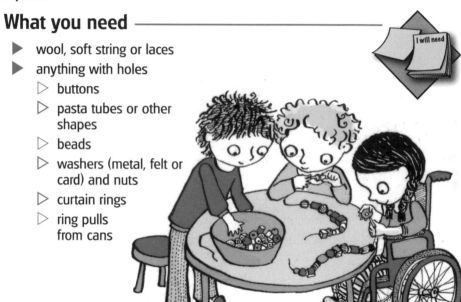

What you do

1. If you are using wool or thread without stiff ends, you can make the activity easier by dipping the ends of the strings in melted wax or wrapping a small strip of masking tape around the end before offering them to the children.

2. Offer the children lots of different sorts of objects with different-sized holes, so they are challenged in making different sorts of strings.

3. Help the children to knot the ends or to put knots between the objects to stop them sliding.

4. Hang the strings in bushes and trees, or use them in role play and celebrations.

And another idea...

▶ Colour some of the pasta shapes by putting them into a ziplock bag with a small amount of food colouring. Shake the bag to distribute the colour, then pour the pasta shapes out on to a paper towel to dry.

▶ Make lots of small shapes cut from card, polystyrene, foil, plastic trays, felt or thicker plastic bags. Punch holes in them and add these to the collection.

▶ Collect natural objects with holes in, such as stones and shells, and add these.

▶ Add pieces from construction sets and other toys.

▶ Buy some soft wire (copper fuse wire is good) and thread beads on short lengths to make decorations for Christmas or other celebrations. This needs careful supervision.

Links with EYFS goals

Physical Development
▶ Demonstrates fine motor control and coordination.
▶ Uses small and large equipment, showing a range of basic skills.

Creative Development
▶ Explores different media and responds to a variety of sensory experiences.
▶ Explores colour, texture, shape, form and space in two or three dimensions

Problem Solving, Reasoning and Numeracy
Shape, space and measures
▶ Talks about, recognises and recreates simple patterns.

First needles – I can sew

'Blunt' needles, made of metal or plastic, are easy to get hold of through educational supply catalogues, or buy darning or weaving needles from a craft shop. Children need to practise using these in simple activities before using them for sewing fabrics together.

What you need

- wool or embroidery threads
- safe needles with big eyes
- polystyrene packing materials – 'wiggles', chips, tubes or squares – bio-degradable ones are more environmentally friendly, as they dissolve in water when you have finished with them. Try to get a variety of shapes and sizes.

What you do

1. Show the children how to thread their needles, or help them if they need it.

2. Make sure there is a knot in the end of the wool or thread.

3. Help the children to push their needles through the polystyrene or other packing materials to make snakes and necklaces.

4. Tie the ends of the wool or thread together, or hang up the string.

5. You could colour the strings and necklaces with paint or felt tips. Don't make bio-degradable beads too wet or they will dissolve!

And another idea...

▶ Buy some peanuts in their shells and thread these. (Be aware of nut allergies). Hang the nuts in the garden to feed the birds.

▶ Cut thick slices of stale bread in squares and bake them in the oven until they are crisp. Use these for threading to make different bird food strings.

▶ In autumn, collect some leaves and thread these on strings.

▶ Cut thin sponge, polystyrene or plastic bags into shapes for threading with a needle.

▶ Make strings of buttons, beads or small pasta shapes, using a needle to help with smaller holes.

Links with EYFS goals

Physical Development

▶ Demonstrates fine motor control and coordination.

▶ Uses small and large equipment, showing a range of basic skills.

Creative Development

▶ Explores different media and responds to a variety of sensory experiences.

▶ Explores colour, texture, shape, form and space in two or three dimensions.

Problem Solving, Reasoning and Numeracy

Shape, space and measures

▶ Talks about, recognises and recreates simple patterns.

Sewing cards – in and out the holes

Simple Sewing cards are a familiar activity for helping with sewing skills. Buy some or make your own.

What you need

- ▶ sturdy card (cereal boxes or other packaging)
- ▶ hole punch (a paper punch or one with varied size holes – see 'Resources and contacts' on page 80)
- ▶ safe needles or laces
- ▶ wool or embroidery threads

What you do

1. The best sort of sewing cards to use first are ones without pictures. Younger children may find it difficult to follow the outline of a drawing, so make these cards from coloured or painted card with holes round the edges or randomly scattered across the card.

2. Let children have free access to these cards. Don't worry if they just keep pushing the needle through from the front.

3. When they have had plenty of practice in free play, show the children how to push the needle through, catch it at the back, then push it back again (this needs some practice!).

4. The next stage – pushing the needle through, then pushing it back again – needs to be demonstrated and supported by an adult.

5. Now you could make some picture or shape cards by drawing outlines, tracing simple pictures from stories or using clip art from your computer. Make sure these pictures are very simple. (Google 'lacing cards' or 'threading cards' to find some downloads.)

And another idea...

▶ If younger children are having difficulty with the cards, get some lacing shapes (cubes, bugs, apples etc.) and let them practise on these first.

▶ Make lacing stars, trees and other shapes for greeting cards, calendars and decorations for festivals.

▶ Make sewing cards with favourite characters from TV and DVD, using children's birthday cards stuck on very thick card. Use a single craft punch or a big nail and a hammer to start the holes.

▶ Buy some plastic or thick sewing cards from an education supply catalogue.

Links with EYFS goals

Personal, Social and Emotional Development

Dispositions and attitudes

▶ Shows an interest in classroom activities through observation or participation.

▶ Displays high levels of involvement in self-chosen activities.

▶ Selects and uses activities and resources independently.

Knowledge and Understanding of the World

▶ Shows curiosity and interest in the features of objects and living things.

▶ Observes, selects and manipulates objects and materials.

Pegs and nails – wind it round

Peg and nail boards are very useful for winding and twisting threads and ribbon. You can buy these from education suppliers or bead shops, or you could make your own from wooden boards and nails. This is an adult job, unless you have very skilful children!

What you need

- ▶ ready-made pegboards
- ▶ or the materials to make them – pieces of wood, nails with big or rounded heads and hammers
- ▶ string, wool or threads in different colours

What you do

1. If you want to make a pegboard, help the children to hammer nails into a board in a regular pattern (following your marks on the board) or in a random pattern – each has its value and attraction.

2. You can display the finished board flat or vertically.

3. Show the children how to make a pattern by winding threads round and between the pegs, making patterns and shapes.

And another idea...

▶ Use polystyrene shapes and make pegboards with pushpins (sometimes called mapping pins). Make sure you choose pins with big heads and thick pieces of polystyrene, such as the packing from electrical goods. Older and more dextrous children will be able to make their own pegboards with these resources.

▶ Make a really big pegboard outside by pushing canes or broom handles into the ground and walking through and round the 'pegs' with ribbons or long strings.

▶ Find some odd socks or tights and cut them across in strips so they are in circles. Use these on pegboards of all sizes, or try elastic bands.

Links with EYFS goals

Knowledge and Understanding of the World

▶ Observes, selects and manipulates objects and materials.

▶ Investigates objects and materials by using all their senses as appropriate (ELG).

Physical Development

▶ Demonstrates fine motor control and coordination.

▶ Uses small and large equipment, showing a range of basic skills (ELG).

▶ Handles tools, objects, construction and malleable materials safely and with basic control (ELG).

Wrapping and binding

Wrapping is a technique where objects are covered all over, using thread, string or strips of fabric. Look on Google at the work of Philippa Lawrence (who wraps trees) or Christo (who wraps buildings and even islands) to see some examples, or print some to talk about.

What you need

▶ old clothes or pieces of fabric (any fabric can be used, but stretchy or knitted fabric works well)

▶ scissors

▶ ribbons, threads, raffia and strings

▶ objects to wrap:
  ▷ sticks and twigs
  ▷ soft toys
  ▷ small world figures
  ▷ bricks and strong cartons

I will need

What you do

1. Look at some pictures of wrapping with the children.

2. Make some strips by cutting or tearing lengths from fabrics of different sorts and colours. Coloured raffia is cheap, pliable and easy to work with, so include some if you can.

3. Now collect some objects to wrap. You may like to start with a group project, wrapping something bigger together, before letting children choose their own objects to wrap. Encourage them to be reasonable about size, but don't stifle children with big ideas!

4. Help the children to wrap the objects they choose. They may need help with starting new strips and fixing the ends.

And another idea...

▶ Try wrapping some unusual objects, such as wheeled toys, furniture or dolls.

▶ Do some wrapping with plaster bandage (from art suppliers). This is messy, but very good fun and the plaster bandage hardens almost immediately.

▶ Try wrapping gifts with fabric.

▶ Take a walk in your local park and do some wrapping while you are there (you should probably ask first!).

Links with EYFS goals

Physical Development

▶ Constructs in a purposeful way, using simple tools and techniques.

▶ Demonstrates fine motor control and coordination.

▶ Uses small and large equipment, showing a range of basic skills.

▶ Handles tools, objects, construction and malleable materials safely and with basic control.

Creative Development

▶ Explores different media and responds to a variety of sensory experiences.

▶ Explores colour, texture, shape, form and space in two or three dimensions.

Stiffening threads with glue – sticky threads

Mixing threads with glue opens up a new range of possibilities. The thread takes on a new quality and holds its shape.

What you need

- ▶ wool, soft string or embroidery thread
- ▶ dilute white glue or cellulose paste
- ▶ ready-mixed paint
- ▶ a plastic sheet or black plastic bag

What you do

1. With the children, cut lots of different lengths of wool and string.
2. Put some dilute PVA or cellulose paste in shallow containers and add colour if you wish.
3. Spread the plastic sheet on a table or the floor.
4. Take single lengths of string etc. and dip them in the glue.
5. Lift each one by the end and put it on the plastic, making shapes or little piles.
6. Leave the plastic sheet somewhere warm until the strings are dry.
7. Now help the children to lift their strings from the plastic. They should have hardened into stringy shapes.

And another idea...

▶ Drape the wet strings over twigs and branches and leave them to dry.

▶ While the string shapes are still wet, sprinkle them with glitter or salt. This will make them sparkle so you can decorate a branch or twig for a display in your room.

▶ Dip strings in glue, then glitter, and put them on black card or paper for greeting cards or calendars.

▶ Have a colour theme, with blue and white, or green and yellow to add to a seasonal display.

▶ Inflate some balloons and wind the wet strings round them. When the strings are dry, deflate the balloon and you should have a string shape to hang up and decorate.

Links with EYFS goals

Knowledge and Understanding of the World

▶ Shows curiosity and interest by exploring surroundings.

▶ Observes, selects and manipulates objects and materials.

▶ Investigates objects and materials by using all their senses as appropriate.

▶ Looks closely at similarities, differences, patterns and change.

Physical Development

▶ Demonstrates fine motor control and coordination.

▶ Uses small and large equipment, showing a range of basic skills.

Tying and ribbons – our lovely fence (1)

Tying ribbons and strings will encourage the development of fine motor control and persistence. It is also a good activity for involving boys, particularly if you choose materials and places carefully.

What you need

▶ ribbons, strings and strips of fabric

▶ plastic bags cut into strips

▶ scissors

▶ places to tie the strings and ribbons:

  ▷ fences, gates and bushes in the garden of your setting

  ▷ plastic-covered fencing (buy a piece and fix it firmly somewhere indoors or outside)

  ▷ bamboo canes or broom handles

What you do

1. Cut the materials into suitable lengths – not too long or they will get tangled, not too short or the children won't be able to tie them.

2. Show the children how to tie them, and where.

3. Stay with them to start with, so you can model and help.

4. Once they have the idea, children will be able to do this activity unaided, and some will get very involved in untying too!

5. Don't forget to keep adding new sorts of materials to keep the activity fresh.

And another idea...

▶ Put up washing lines or ropes for tying to make screens and dividers indoors and outside.

▶ Offer some hoops for ribbon tying and use these as wind dancers outside.

▶ Practise tying to make ribbons for soft toys and dolls, leads for toy dogs etc.

▶ Use ribbons to hang sound makers in your garden.

Links with EYFS goals

Personal, Social and Emotional Development

Dispositions and attitudes

▶ Displays high levels of involvement in self-chosen activities.

▶ Selects and uses activities and resources independently.

Physical Development

▶ Demonstrates fine motor control and coordination.

▶ Uses small and large equipment, showing a range of basic skills.

Creative Development

▶ Explores different media and responds to a variety of sensory experiences.

▶ Explores colour, texture, shape, form and space in two or three dimensions.

Winding and threading – pompoms and tassels

Making pompoms is a simple but fascinating activity, and can produce balls for other toys and figures.

What you need

▶ lots of colours of wool (try markets or craft shops)
▶ strong card
▶ scissors

What you do

1. Cut some circles of card, about 10cm across.
2. Make a hole in the middle of each circle about 2cm across.
3. Cut some lengths of wool about 30cm long.
4. Put two circles together and help the children wind wool through the hole and round the two circles of card, changing colour when they want to.
5. Continue until the card is so full that the child can't push any more wool through the middle.
6. Now carefully cut the wool round the edge of the card, slipping the scissor blades between the two circles of card. Then slide a piece of wool firmly between the two pieces of card to secure the wool. Until children are very confident, this should be done by an adult!
7. Pull the two pieces of card off the woolly ball and fluff it up so you can't see the tied wool in the middle. The pompoms are great for indoor games – aiming, tossing and catching.

And another idea...

▶ Make your pompom into a pet by adding some googly eyes or:

▷ some ears

▷ a tail

▷ whiskers

▷ hair

▶ Attach some thin elastic to make a bouncy ball.

▶ Make more pompoms of different sizes to make animals – rabbits, cats, teddies etc.

▶ Use bright, deep colours to make superhero balls for Superman, Spiderman and others.

▶ Learn how to make tassels using two rectangles of card. Put the two rectangles together, wind wool round and round, cut along one long side of the card and tie the lengths together. Then tie again round all the lengths, just below the first tie. Attach a string or cord and hang up for decoration or to make something work. Or make some in superhero colours and thread on elastic to make superhero wristbands with tassels!

Links with EYFS goals

Personal, Social and Emotional Development

Dispositions and attitudes

▶ Continues to be interested, motivated and excited to learn.

▶ Is confident to try new activities, initiate ideas and speak in a familiar group.

▶ Maintains attention and concentrates.

Physical Development

▶ Constructs in a purposeful way, using simple tools and techniques.

▶ Demonstrates fine motor control and coordination.

Twisting and plaiting – twisty!

Twisting is a simple version of plaiting and is a good introduction to making cords and strings. You can sew or tie tassels to the ends to finish them off.

What you need

▶ wool, soft string or raffia

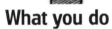

What you do

1. This activity is just about twisting lengths of string or wool together to make ropes or cords.

2. Start with a length of string or wool and loop the middle of the length over a chair or hook.

3. Tie the ends of the wool together.

4. Put your hand or finger in the loop and twist the wool by winding it round and round so it twists round itself.

5. As the twist gets tighter, you will be able to double the wool or string to make a thicker cord.

6. Tie the ends of the double twist together and they will stay.

7. Use the cord to make a belt, bracelet or headband.

And another idea...

▶ Make longer twists to use as light pulls.

▶ Add beads or other items to the twists and plaits.

▶ Make a very long twist to use as a decorative line for hanging pictures or objects.

▶ Experiment with plaiting. Tie the ends of three pieces of wool together and hook them over a cup hook screwed into the wall. Let the children experiment with winding and weaving the three lengths together. Older or more dextrous children may be able to learn to plait more formally.

▶ Make a doll with very long hair made from wool and practise plaiting the hair.

▶ See if you can find someone who knows how to do hair braiding or plaiting. Ask them to come and show the children how it is done.

▶ Use much thicker cord to make a rope.

Links with EYFS goals

Knowledge and Understanding of the World

▶ Observes, selects and manipulates objects and materials.

▶ Investigates objects and materials by using all their senses as appropriate.

▶ Looks closely at similarities, differences, patterns and change.

Physical Development

▶ Constructs in a purposeful way, using simple tools and techniques.

▶ Demonstrates fine motor control and coordination.

Natural weaving – our lovely fence (2)

Use natural materials or places in your setting to begin to experiment with weaving.

What you need

▶ a fence or trellis, or buy a piece of garden fencing (green plastic, willow, wood or plastic-covered sorts work well)

▶ strips of fabric, plastic bags cut into strips and ends of ribbon (try your local florist)

▶ natural materials, such as leaves, feathers, stones, seeds and twigs

▶ string and wool for hanging objects

What you do

1. Show the children how to tie the strips of fabric or plastic through the fence, or weave them in and out of a fence.

2. Let them experiment independently with fixing, tying and weaving, giving help to those who need it.

3. Photograph their work and talk about how it was made.

4. Offer some natural objects to incorporate in their work.

And another idea...

▶ Try indoor weaving using different sorts of paper and card, by recycling junk mail, wrapping paper on a piece of plastic fencing or netting hung from the ceiling.

▶ Go for a seasonal walk and make a seasonal hanging.

▶ Collect some bare branches and wind wool or string between the twigs. Add some seeds, leaves and other objects.

▶ Make a festive hanging by adding sequins, beads and glittery wool.

▶ Make a bird hanging by incorporating strings of nuts, twigs of berries and seed heads.

Links with EYFS goals

Knowledge and Understanding of the World

▶ Shows curiosity and interest by exploring surroundings.

▶ Observes, selects and manipulates objects and materials.

▶ Investigates objects and materials by using all their senses as appropriate.

▶ Looks closely at similarities, differences, patterns and change.

Creative Development

▶ Explores different media and responds to a variety of sensory experiences.

▶ Explores colour, texture, shape, form and space in two or three dimensions.

▶ Uses imagination in art and design.

▶ Responds in a variety of ways to what they see, hear, smell, touch and feel.

Simple looms – make a weaving

Making simple looms with the children will extend their experience with weaving. They require some concentration, so it's better to start with a group or class effort so lots of children can contribute.

What you need

▶ an old picture frame or wooden box to make the loom (ask a greengrocer for a box or look in charity shops for old pictures in frames)

▶ string

▶ a hammer, some small pliers and some nails

▶ wool, thin fabric strips, ribbons and braid

I will need

What you do

1. Help the children to make the loom by hammering nails into two of the sides of the box or frame. Use the pliers to hold each nail as they hammer it in (this will help to avoid banged fingers!). The nails should be secure, but still sticking up, and about 5cm apart, but don't be too fussy!

2. When the nails are secure, help the children to wind the string from side to side, round the nails, to make the warp of the loom. You should end up with a pattern of parallel lines across the loom.

3. Now show the children how to weave the wool or other strips under and over the strings. It's best to start with shorter lengths so they just go across the loom once. This will avoid tangling and frustration. The ends will provide a decorative fringing.

4. You could use shades of the same colour or just let a random pattern evolve as children add new colours and textures.

5. When the loom is as full as you can make it, you should be able to slip the strings off the nails to see your completed hanging.

And another idea...

▶ Tie vegetable or fruit nets to pieces of card and offer thinner wool and string.

▶ Make a card loom (or smaller looms) from pieces of thick card (such as the sides of cartons). Cut deep 'V'-shaped notches in two sides of the card and use string to make the warp threads. Children could then weave their own mats or hangings, or use them to make cards or other gifts.

▶ Make seasonal weavings by restricting the colours or textures, and adding other objects, such as beads, ring pulls or other recycled objects.

Links with EYFS goals

Personal, Social and Emotional Development
Dispositions and attitudes
▶ Selects and uses activities and resources independently.

▶ Continues to be interested, motivated and excited to learn.

▶ Is confident to try new activities, initiate ideas and speak in a familiar group.

▶ Maintains attention and concentrates.

Social development
▶ Works as part of a group or class, taking turns and sharing fairly (ELG).

▶ Takes into account the ideas of others.

Creative Development
▶ Explores different media and responds to a variety of sensory experiences.

▶ Explores colour, texture, shape, form and space in two or three dimensions.

▶ Uses imagination in art and design.

▶ Responds in a variety of ways to what they see, hear, smell, touch and feel.

Paper weaving – in and out again

Weaving with paper is a familiar and well-used activity that helps children to understand how weaving works, using simple and manageable resources.

What you need

▶ strong paper in several different colours

▶ scissors

▶ a pen or pencil

What you do

1. Start by cutting some squares of strong paper (about 30cm wide).

2. Fold the squares in half and draw lines from the fold towards the edge at regular intervals of 3cm apart. Don't go too close to the edges of the paper.

3. Let the children cut along the lines, helping them if they need it.

4. Unfold the paper square – it should have cuts almost all the way across.

5. Now cut some strips of contrasting colours, about 2.5cm wide and 30cm long.

6. Show the children how to weave these strips in and out of the slots in the paper. They need to go under and over, and to start each new strip so it alternates with the last one to make a pattern of colours.

And another idea...

▶ Cut some different shapes for paper weaving – rectangles, hearts and circles – and weave in and out of these.

▶ Use magazine pages with big photos on them as bases for paper weaving, either weaving strips from another photo through the sheet, or using a single colour for the strips. This will give a great look to the photo.

▶ Cut wiggly lines across the base sheet and thread wiggly strips through them.

▶ Try using some more unusual papers and card – foil, wrapping paper and plastic carrier bags.

▶ Work with the children to paint patterns on sheets of paper and cut these for big paper weaving projects.

Links with EYFS goals

Knowledge and Understanding of the World

▶ Observes, selects and manipulates objects and materials.

▶ Investigates objects and materials by using all their senses as appropriate.

▶ Looks closely at similarities, differences, patterns and change.

Physical Development

▶ Constructs in a purposeful way, using simple tools and techniques.

▶ Demonstrates fine motor control and coordination.

▶ Uses small and large equipment, showing a range of basic skills.

▶ Handles tools, objects, construction and malleable materials safely and with basic control.

Binca and canvas – more in and out patterns

Binca is a stiff canvas fabric with an open weave, specially produced for sewing. You can get it from education catalogues. Other fabrics with open weaves can also be used for simple sewing activities. These include embroidery canvas, hessian and open weave fabrics, such as nets.

What you need

- open weave fabric pieces about 30cm across
- blunt-ended needles (metal or plastic) – you can get these from education suppliers or craft shops
- needle threaders (from a craft shop) – these will make threading easier for the children and for you!
- wool or embroidery cottons in different colours
- scissors

What you do

1. Show the children the resources.
2. Cut some pieces of thread or wool (not too long) and help them to thread their needles (showing them how to use a needle threader may save you all some time).
3. Tie a knot in the end of the cotton or wool to avoid frustration.
4. Now just let them have a go at sewing. It doesn't matter if their first attempts are untidy and they forget to push the needle back through the fabric. This is part of the learning process.

5. Sit with them and do some sewing yourself, with the same resources as they are using. This modelling, especially if you talk about what you are doing as you sew, will really help. Say things like 'I'm pushing the needle through and catching it on the other side. Now I'm pushing it back to the front again.'

And another idea...

▶ When the sewing is done, let the children add sequins and other decorations, sticking them with PVA or a fabric adhesive.

▶ Let the children draw a simple shape or picture on the Binca or other hessian before they start, so they can follow the line with their sewing. This sometimes helps with establishing the front and the back of their work as they push and pull the needle through.

▶ Try to get some potato or vegetable sacks to cut up or use for a group stitching project where children add a piece over time.

▶ Offer some glittery thread or some unusual colours. Look for unusual ones on market stalls or in craft shop bargain bins.

▶ As the children get more confident, offer them some beads or sequins with big holes to thread on the needle as they stitch. These can become part of the creation.

Links with EYFS goals

Personal, Social and Emotional Development
Dispositions and attitudes

▶ Selects and uses activities and resources independently.

▶ Continues to be interested, motivated and excited to learn.

▶ Is confident to try new activities, initiate ideas and speak in a familiar group.

▶ Maintains attention and concentrates.

Physical Development

▶ Demonstrates fine motor control and coordination.

▶ Uses small and large equipment, showing a range of basic skills.

▶ Handles tools, objects, construction and malleable materials safely and with basic control.

▶ Demonstrates coordination and control in large and small movements, and in using tools and equipment.

Wool and Needles – sewing practice

Sewing on strong paper or plastic is an early way to practise simple stitching. A pad under the sewing helps.

What you need

- shapes cut from plastic carrier bags (coloured plastic adds to the variety) or strong paper (brown wrapping paper works really well)
- blunt-ended needles (metal or plastic) – from education suppliers or craft shops
- needle threaders (from a craft shop) – these will make threading easier for the children and for you!
- smooth wool or embroidery cottons in different colours
- scissors
- polystyrene tiles, pieces of sponge or small cushions

What you do

1. Cut some shapes from paper or plastic – the children could help with this. Make sure there are plenty of different shapes and sorts to choose from.
2. Help the children to thread their needles.
3. Put a piece of polystyrene or sponge under the paper or fabric, so the children can push their needle down through the paper or fabric and into the sponge or polystyrene underneath.
4. Lift the paper/plastic to pull the needle through.
5. Turn the paper or plastic over to push the needle back.
6. Continue in this way to make a stitching.

And another idea...

▶ Spray some of the brown paper with gold or silver spray to make festive stitchings.

▶ Fix the completed stitchings on to a big piece of fabric to make a hanging.

▶ Try using black bin bags and shiny threads, then sprinkle glitter on the completed work.

▶ Stitch through more than one layer of plastic or paper and see what happens.

▶ Stitch right through the sponge or polystyrene to incorporate it into the creation, making a double-layered creation.

Links with EYFS goals

Personal, Social and Emotional Development
Dispositions and attitudes

▶ Shows an interest in classroom activities through observation or participation.

▶ Selects and uses activities and resources independently.

▶ Is confident to try new activities, initiate ideas and speak in a familiar group.

▶ Maintains attention and concentrates.

▶ Sustains involvement and perseveres, particularly when trying to solve a problem or reach a satisfactory conclusion.

Physical Development

▶ Demonstrates fine motor control and coordination.

▶ Uses small and large equipment, showing a range of basic skills.

▶ Handles tools, objects, construction and malleable materials safely and with basic control.

▶ Demonstrates coordination and control in large and small movements, and in using tools and equipment.

Hangings with natural objects – hoopla hangings

Make hoops, wheels and fabrics into works of art by stitching, tying and threading natural and man-made objects.

What you need

- a hoop, a bicycle wheel or an umbrella frame with the fabric removed
- lots of things with holes – stones, shells, seeds, washers, paper clips, beads, sequins, counters and pasta
- natural objects to thread and bind – different sorts and sizes of leaves that are easy to sew and thread, twigs and small cones

- strips of fabric (thin fabric is best)
- strips of plastic from bread bags or carrier bags
- thin string, wool, threads and needles
- glue and spreaders
- scissors

What you do

1. Decide what you will use as a base for this work. You may want to involve the children in the choice, or decide yourself.

2. Collect all the resources and look at them together. Take your time and let the children really explore all the objects.

3. Talk about how you might work together to turn the things into a decoration for your setting or your garden.

4. Talk about how you could use the chosen base. It might be a good idea to hang it up securely where the children can work on it, either standing or sitting.

5. Work out a way to cover the frame with plastic or fabric strips. Some children may suggest other methods, such as painting.

6. Now let the children have some free time with all the objects, hanging, stitching, wrapping, tying and threading objects onto the frame, using needles to thread objects, string to tie them, and glue to bind and attach them. They could loop string across the frame, wrap ribbons round it and bind objects to it.

7. Try not to be too insistent on your own ideas of what looks good – let the children create their own thing.

And another idea...

▶ Find some more unusual objects to decorate and turn into works of art. You could use a bike, an old chair, a gold picture frame or a big baby doll.

▶ Wrap your climbing frame, using strips of bread bags and plastic carriers cut into strips.

▶ Make a 'wigwam' with canes and wrap this structure with ribbons, braid, fabric and other decorations.

▶ Make a big hanging/sewing on a 2-metre length of fabric and hang it from a broom handle, indoors or outside.

▶ Turn your hanging into a floral decoration by adding plastic, fabric or real flowers, leaves and fruit.

Links with EYFS goals

Personal, Social and Emotional Development
Dispositions and attitudes

▶ Shows an interest in classroom activities through observation or participation.

▶ Selects and uses activities and resources independently.

▶ Is confident to try new activities, initiate ideas and speak in a familiar group.

Social development

▶ Works as part of a group or class, taking turns and sharing fairly (ELG).

▶ Takes into account the ideas of others.

Problem Solving, Reasoning and Numeracy
Shape, space and measures

▶ Describes shapes in simple models, pictures and patterns.

▶ Uses everyday words to describe position.

Felt – feel this!

Felt is an easy, no-fray fabric for first fabric work. It comes in an endless array of colours and several thicknesses.

What you need

- ▶ felt in as many colours as you can find – try craft shops and education catalogues, where you can sometimes get bargain packs
- ▶ hessian or other fabric for backing the children's pictures
- ▶ sharp scissors for children to use
- ▶ fabric glue
- ▶ needles and threads
- ▶ sequins and other decorative bits
- ▶ fine felt markers

What you do

1. Show the children how they can cut out shapes from the felt – marking them out first if they want to. You may need to help younger children until they get the hang of cutting this material. Offering them thinner felt sometimes helps.

2. As the children cut their shapes, offer some backing squares or rectangles of hessian or other plain fabric to use as a background for their pattern or picture.

3. Arranging and rearranging the shapes is an important part of the process – don't encourage the children to stick the shapes down too soon, as they may change their minds as they add more to the picture.

4. Use the activity as an opportunity to talk about the shapes, the emerging pictures and the process itself.

5. Once each child is happy with their creation, provide some glue and spreaders. Remind them to be sparing with the glue so it doesn't spoil their picture. Offer a damp cloth for wiping sticky fingers during this stage.

6. Add decorations and details with felt pens, sequins, beads, little buttons etc.

7. Hang the finished pictures on short canes with decorative string attached.

And another idea...

▶ Make 'fuzzy felt' games by covering sturdy card with felt and then cutting shapes and objects out to arrange on the card. The felt will attach itself to the background without glue, enabling children to move and rearrange the pieces. This is a good idea for making repeated patterns or retelling familiar stories.

▶ Cut felt shapes in pairs and stick them together with a string trapped between the two shapes. Decorate these and hang them on a branch or the frame of an umbrella.

▶ Work as a whole group to use the offcuts and spare pieces of felt in a simple creative activity of sticking, curling and arranging, to make an abstract creation on a big piece of fabric backing. Add feathers, shells, leaves etc.

▶ Try paper-backed felt, which you can get from craft shops or DIY stores where it is sold for wall covering. This is sometimes easier to cut, but may be limited in colour, so you will need to provide plenty of decorative bits too.

▶ Self-adhesive felt and foam are other options. These are paper backed and the paper peels off to reveal the glue. Some children may find this material easier to manage.

Links with EYFS goals

Problem Solving, Reasoning and Numeracy
Shape, space and measures
▶ Describes shapes in simple models, pictures and patterns.
▶ Talks about, recognises and recreates simple patterns.

Knowledge and Understanding of the World
▶ Observes, selects and manipulates objects and materials.
▶ Investigates objects and materials by using all their senses as appropriate.

Fabric scraps and strips – make a little person

Thin strips of fabric can provide inspiration for projects without cutting. This may be easier and more instant for some children.

What you need

▶ thin fabrics in a range of colours and patterns – shirts, sari fabric, cotton dresses, skirts and shirt fabric; thicker fabrics are not suitable for this activity

▶ sharp scissors

▶ PVA glue, diluted with water

▶ lolly sticks or twigs

▶ elastic bands

▶ beads, sequins, lace, ribbon, and wool

What you do

1. This activity is quicker if you start by cutting or tearing thin strips of fabric. You may have some children who want to help with this, and it's a very good activity for working off frustration and energy! If you make little cuts in the edge of fabric (about 2cm apart), this will make the tearing much easier.

2. Help the children to bind together two sticks to make a simple stick figure. Elastic bands will make this easier.

3. Now the children can dress their figure with the strips of fabric, winding them round the sticks to make legs, feet, body and arms. Make sure the children use plenty of glue to secure the fabric strips – it may look messy when it's wet, but the glue will dry clear and it will help to make the structure stronger.

4. Some children may want to make a head by capturing a piece of cotton wool in a small square of fabric and securing it with an elastic band to the top of the stick. Draw features with a felt pen and use wool for hair.

5. Offer plenty of decorative bits for those children who want them.

6. A damp cloth for hand wiping is very useful to remove glue from fingers while working.

7. The children could use their people for puppet shows, small world creations, storytelling or just as friends.

And another idea...

▶ Make characters for familiar and favourite stories, and use them to help with recall and retelling.

▶ Make some animals, birds or fantastic creatures by binding sticks together and adding fur, leather or feathers to the strips of fabric. Do the fabric strips first to make the bodies, so the heavier fabrics have something to stick to. Add glass beads for eyes, and cut claws and beaks from plastic pots or tough plastic bags.

▶ Work together to make a decorative tree by wrapping a branch in strips of gluey fabric. Then decorate for a celebration with smaller twigs and other natural objects, such as cones.

Links with EYFS goals

Physical Development

▶ Constructs in a purposeful way, using simple tools and techniques.

▶ Demonstrates fine motor control and coordination.

▶ Uses small and large equipment, showing a range of basic skills.

▶ Handles tools, objects, construction and malleable materials safely and with basic control.

▶ Demonstrates coordination and control in large and small movements, and in using tools and equipment.

Creative Development

▶ Explores different media and responds to a variety of sensory experiences.

▶ Tries to capture experiences, using a variety of different media.

▶ Explores colour, texture, shape, form and space in two or three dimensions.

▶ Uses imagination in art and design.

▶ Responds in a variety of ways to what they see, hear, smell, touch and feel.

Stuffing – make a snake

Stuffing fabric containers with paper is a very simple way to make 3D objects very quickly. Children love these experiences because they have an instant appeal.

What you need

- tights, either children's or adults'
  - make sure they are thick enough to take the stuffing without tearing
- plenty of newspaper or paper shreddings
- thread
- paint and brushes
- decorations such as felt and beads etc.

- pictures of snakes

I will need

What you do

1. Each child needs a leg of a pair of tights to make a snake, so cut the body part off and cut it into strips for stuffing.

2. Now get each child to stuff as much screwed-up paper into their snake as they can.

3. When the snake is full, help the children to tie the end of the snake so the stuffing is secure.

4. Now talk about what snakes look like – looking at some pictures or books together to check patterns, eyes, colours etc.

5. Look at the decorative objects you have collected and help the children to select the things they want to use to decorate their own snake. Some may want to use paint or felt pens, others may want to use sequins or braid. Felt is useful for tongues, and glass beads make great eyes – or you could provide some 'googly' eyes.

6. When the snakes are decorated and dry, the children could attach strings to them so they can use them as puppets, or hang them up for display.

And another idea...

▶ Collect lots of plastic carrier bags and cut them into strips for recycled stuffing.

▶ Stuff a whole set of clothes to make a scarecrow. Use a broom handle and stuff some trousers (or jeans), a sweatshirt and some gloves for hands. Make a head by stuffing a plastic carrier bag with paper and tying the opening closed. Decorate with paint and PVA mixed together, and add some hair and a hat. Put your scarecrow in the garden of your setting and make it the focus for songs and stories.

▶ Stuff some old pillowcases, stitch, glue or tie the ends shut and decorate them to make some cushions for your book area. Or stuff some big plastic bags for waterproof outdoor cushions.

▶ Stuff some tights to make draught stoppers.

Links with EYFS goals

Communication, Language and Literacy
Reading

▶ Shows an understanding of how information can be found in non-fiction texts to answer questions about where, who, why and how.

Physical Development

▶ Constructs in a purposeful way, using simple tools and techniques.

▶ Demonstrates fine motor control and coordination.

▶ Uses small and large equipment, showing a range of basic skills.

Creative Development

▶ Explores different media and responds to a variety of sensory experiences.

▶ Tries to capture experiences using a variety of different media.

▶ Explores colour, texture, shape, form and space in two or three dimensions.

▶ Uses imagination in art and design.

▶ Responds in a variety of ways to what they see, hear, smell, touch and feel.

Fabric collage and pictures – scrap pictures

Get children used to being creative with scraps of fabric by making scrap pictures and hanging them up.

What you need

- a variety of fabrics cut or torn into pieces, strips and shapes
- hessian, denim or other thicker woven fabric for the backing
- PVA glue
- scissors
- threads and decorations
- sticks, twigs or chopsticks to make the frames
- needles

I will need

What you do

1. When children first get involved in this less structured activity, some may need some help to create something from nothing. Sit with them so you can talk with them about how they could use the fabrics to make their own picture or design. You could model the activity by making your own picture, but try not to imply that yours is the 'right' way.

2. It's a good idea to choose the background first.

3. Children can then add fabric pieces to enhance the background – adding pieces to make sky, sea, fields, gardens etc.

4. Once they are happy with their background, they can enhance it with smaller pieces of fabric to make the details of their picture. Sharp scissors and sometimes a bit of adult help will make this a more satisfying experience.

5. When the children are happy with their pictures, help them to make a frame by sticking four sticks to the edge, and tying some thread or string to the ends of one stick to hang them up.

And another idea...

▶ Use the children's pictures to make covers for scrapbooks, by slipping them into a display book and filling the book with photos of children's sewing, fabric work and other activities. You could also make themed books of photos with colour coded or appropriate fabric pictures on the front.

▶ Get some cushion pads and use the children's fabric pictures to decorate them by sewing or sticking them onto the pads. Use these in your book areas and for outside activities, and replace them when they get worn.

▶ Make small fabric pictures for greeting cards or calendars. Limit the range of colours or the decorations you offer according to the season or event.

▶ Make a great big fabric collage by putting a sheet or a shower curtain on a table or on the floor and working together on the picture. Hang the finished picture up as a screen or curtain in your setting.

Links with EYFS goals

Knowledge and Understanding of the World

▶ Shows curiosity and interest by exploring surroundings.

▶ Observes, selects and manipulates objects and materials.

▶ Investigates objects and materials by using all their senses as appropriate.

Creative Development

▶ Explores different media and responds to a variety of sensory experiences.

▶ Tries to capture experiences using a variety of different media.

▶ Explores colour, texture, shape, form and space in two or three dimensions.

▶ Uses imagination in art and design.

▶ Responds in a variety of ways to what they see, hear, smell, touch and feel.

Scarves, masks and headscarves – bandannas and superheroes

Simple fabric pieces for dressing up are the start of making your own costumes and clothes. These simple shapes are versatile and good fun for indoor or outdoor play.

What you need

- cotton or thin-knitted fabric in plain colours or patterns (spots, stripes, flowers etc.) – make sure you have some plain fabric and a mixture of pastel and deep colours (red and dark blue will appeal to many boys, pastel colours may well appeal to girls)
- sharp scissors
- felt pens
- a big mirror

What you do

1. You may like to do this activity in or near your role-play area or outside, so the children can add other resources to the ones they make.

2. Talk with the children about who might wear the different sorts of fabrics. Think about story, film and TV characters as well as familiar workers or sports people. Of course, children will naturally think of superhero capes and masks, but you could introduce some of the following:

   ▷ protective work headgear for waiters, chefs' hats and other headwear for fast food places
   ▷ hairnets and hats for food preparation and supermarkets

▷ the protective headgear that doctors, surgeons and nurses wear

▷ hair bands and headbands for decoration and for sports

▷ bandannas

▷ cowboy scarves and other neckerchiefs

▷ wristbands with badges or names for sports or charities

▷ historical headdresses

▷ fabric headdresses and scarves from different cultures and countries.

And another idea...

▶ Use fabric to make shawls, cloaks and capes. Decorate these with braid, ribbons, metallic paint or even fake jewels.

▶ Make aprons for different activities. Cut apron shapes from plain fabric and attach strings or straps by tying, clipping or sewing. Decorate the aprons with words and pictures for activities, such as cooking, woodwork, craft, gardening etc. or personalise them for each child by naming them and drawing pictures.

Links with EYFS goals

Personal, Social and Emotional Development
Social development
▶ Works as part of a group or class, taking turns and sharing fairly (ELG).
▶ Takes into account the ideas of others.

Creative Development

▶ Explores different media and responds to a variety of sensory experiences.

▶ Explores colour, texture, shape, form and space in two or three dimensions.

▶ Uses imagination in art and design.

▶ Responds in a variety of ways to what they see, hear, smell, touch and feel.

▶ Expresses and communicates ideas, thoughts and feelings using a range of materials, suitable tools, imaginative role-play, movement, designing and making, and a variety of songs and musical instruments.

Fringing – make a mat

Pulling threads from the edges or the middle of fabrics is a really satisfying activity. Some children will continue to pull until they have nothing left but a pile of threads!

What you need

▶ fabric with a loose, open weave – hessian or woven netting, such as net curtains

▶ children's needles

▶ plastic tweezers

▶ scissors

▶ coloured threads, thin ribbons, wool and felt pens

▶ magnifying glasses

What you do

1. Cut the hems and selvedge (the machine-finished edge) from the fabrics so they are easy to fringe or thread, and cut the fabric into manageable pieces.

2. Use magnifying glasses to look closely at the fabrics and talk about what you see. Talk about how the threads run across each other to make the fabric strong.

3. Now let the children choose which piece of fabric they will work with and use a magnifying glass to look at the edges of their piece.

4. Help them to get hold of a thread to pull from one edge of the fabric, with their fingers or a pair of tweezers.

5. Work round the piece of fabric, pulling a thread from each edge in turn, until the fabric has a satisfying fringe all round.

6. Now make the creation into a mat by:
- ▷ Drawing a picture in the middle.
- ▷ Adding decorative objects, such as sequins or beads.
- ▷ Sewing a picture.

And another idea...

▶ When children are used to fringing, you could explore pulling threads from the middle of the piece. Fringe the piece first, then pick up one of the threads from the fringe and pull – it should pull out right across the piece of fabric, leaving a little path. Pull out a few more threads, either next to the first one or somewhere else, to make a pattern of pulled threads. Don't get carried away or you will end up with a pile of threads and no fabric! These drawn-thread patterns look lovely displayed on a contrasting colour.

▶ Make a big drawn-thread work and fringed tablecloth for your snack table or for picnics.

▶ Make scarves by fringing the ends of long pieces of fabric.

Links with EYFS goals

Personal, Social and Emotional Development
Dispositions and attitudes
▶ Selects and uses activities and resources independently.

▶ Continues to be interested, motivated and excited to learn.

▶ Is confident to try new activities, initiate ideas and speak in a familiar group.

▶ Maintains attention and concentrates.

▶ Sustains involvement and perseveres, particularly when trying to solve a problem or reach a satisfactory conclusion.

Physical Development

▶ Demonstrates fine motor control and coordination.

▶ Handles tools, objects, construction and malleable materials safely and with basic control.

▶ Demonstrates coordination and control in large and small movements, and in using tools and equipment.

Tie dye – tie together, dye together

Tie-dye doesn't have to be messy or difficult. It is quite suitable for younger children as long as you adapt the materials and the method.

What you need

▶ a big piece of white or light coloured cotton fabric – a cotton sheet is ideal

▶ small waterproof objects to tie in – Lego, big beads, Unfix cubes, big buttons, smooth pebbles, plastic toys etc.

▶ lots of elastic bands

▶ food colouring

(get big bottles from education suppliers) or cold water dye, such as Brusho

▶ rubber gloves for the adult

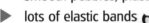

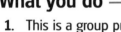

What you do

1. This is a group project that may take several days to complete. Try to involve all the children, even if they only do one object. It is also very good practice for fine motor skills.

2. Talk with the children about what you are going to do, and demonstrate how to fix the objects in the fabric with the elastic bands. You could do a single sample in a small piece of fabric, so they can see what happens.

3. Now put the big piece of fabric in the middle of the floor (this is the best place to do it) and show the children all the different sorts of objects they could enclose. You could let them find some more, but you need to explain the importance of using things that are waterproof.

4. The children will soon get used to manipulating the objects and the elastic bands – although some will find it easier than others. Remind them to get each elastic band as tight as they can.

5. When the children have tied as many objects as they can fit in the fabric, or when they have had enough of the activity, you are ready for the dying.

6. Fill a big container, such as a water tray, with water and add some food colouring or cold-water dye. Stir so it is thoroughly mixed.

7. Add the tied fabric and keep it submerged by poking it with sticks or swishing it with your hands, but wear rubber gloves or it will stain your hands. Putting heavy things like bricks or tins of paint in plastic carrier bags on top of the fabric will help to weight it down.

8. Leave the fabric for several hours or follow the instructions for the cold-water dye.

9. Now take the fabric out of the dye bath and put it in clean water, changing this until it runs clear. Let the children watch all these processes; they are important parts of the activity.

10. When the water is clear, lift the fabric out to drain.

11. You don't need to wait until the fabric is dry to reveal the pattern. Just put it back in the empty water tray and show the children how they can take off the elastic bands to reveal the amazing pattern.

12. Hang your creation out to dry.

Links with EYFS goals

Personal, Social and Emotional Development
Dispositions and attitudes
▶ Shows an interest in classroom activities through observation or participation.

▶ Selects and uses activities and resources independently.

▶ Continues to be interested, motivated and excited to learn.

▶ Is confident to try new activities, initiate ideas and speak in a familiar group.

▶ Maintains attention and concentrates.

▶ Sustains involvement and perseveres, particularly when trying to solve a problem or reach a satisfactory conclusion.

Social development
▶ Works as part of a group or class, taking turns and sharing fairly.

▶ Takes into account the ideas of others.

Physical Development
▶ Demonstrates fine motor control and coordination.

▶ Uses small and large equipment, showing a range of basic skills.

▶ Handles tools, objects, construction and malleable materials safely and with basic control.

▶ Demonstrates coordination and control in large and small movements, and in using tools and equipment.

Stiffening fabric – easy-cut decorations

Stiffening thinner fabrics by using glue is a useful way of making them easier to work with.

What you need

- thin fabrics, such as voile, net, gauze, nylon and thin cotton
- plastic sheeting or black bin liners
- PVA diluted with water, and brushes
- sharp scissors
- craft scissors with patterned blades
- thin, decorative string

What you do

1. Cut the fabrics into pieces about the size of the palm of a child's hand. Let them help!

2. Now spread plastic sheet or an opened-out bin liner on a table.

3. Show the children how to stick the fabric pieces on the plastic, using the glue and brushes (these are easier than spreaders for this activity). They should cover the plastic entirely with no gaps, but it doesn't matter if the pieces overlap, as this will make the finished piece stronger.

4. When the plastic is covered, paint over the whole thing with more glue to stick down any corners. Don't worry if it looks messy – the glue will dry clear.

5. Leave the whole thing to dry completely.

6. Help the children to peel the fabric off the plastic and you will have a sheet of multicoloured fabric, which is easy to cut and bend.

7. Use plain or decorative scissors to cut shapes, make pictures, use string on threads to make decorations, or cover windows and display areas.

And another idea...

▶ Find or buy some lacy fabric. Use the same method to stiffen it and then cut the lacy shapes out for snowflake or Christmas decorations. You could colour the lace while it is still wet with glue by using water-based markers or fabric dyes.

▶ Make a transparent den or tent by making a big piece of this fabric and draping it over a rope, a table or from hooks on your climbing frame. Or hang the piece horizontally over a corner of your room for a magical roof.

▶ Make capes and wings for role play by cutting suitable sizes and attaching elastic to go round shoulders and wrists.

Links with EYFS goals

Knowledge and Understanding of the World

▶ Shows curiosity and interest by exploring surroundings.

▶ Observes, selects and manipulates objects and materials.

▶ Investigates objects and materials by using all their senses as appropriate.

▶ Looks closely at similarities, differences, patterns and change.

Creative Development

▶ Explores different media and responds to a variety of sensory experiences.

▶ Tries to capture experiences using a variety of different media.

▶ Explores colour, texture, shape, form and space in two or three dimensions.

▶ Uses imagination in art and design.

▶ Responds in a variety of ways to what they see, hear, smell, touch and feel.

Banners, flags and streamers – make a windsock

Using fabric to make flags and other decorations is a really quick way to engage everyone in a festival or celebration.

What you need

- a piece of lightweight fabric, about 3 metres/2.5 yards long and about 1 metre/3/4 yard wide (sheeting, net curtain, voile or nylon would be perfect)
- patterned and plain fabric scraps of all sorts
- paint and brushes
- glue
- sharp children's scissors
- a stapler
- string or thin rope
- a hoop
- some duct tape or a needle and thread

- a place to fix your windsock, such as a hook, fence or tree branch, or even the top of your climbing frame

What you do

1. Look up 'windsock' on Google images or another search engine, and look at the pictures before you start.
2. Put the fabric on the floor indoors or outside, and talk about the different ways you could decorate it – paint, fabric strips, shapes, letters and braid. You could even personalise it to your setting.
3. Help the children to decorate the windsock in the ways they have chosen.
4. When the decorations are dry, staple or stitch the long edges together.

5. Now fix the top of the windsock to the hoop by sewing it firmly or sticking it with silver duct tape. The windsock will need to be firmly fixed, particularly if your setting is somewhere windy.

6. Now poke three holes in the fabric near the hoop and equally spaced round it, and attach strings round the hoop at these places.

7. To fly the windsock, attach it firmly to a pole or another suitable place in your outdoor area.

And another idea...

▶ Cut or tear fabric into strips for streamers, or triangles for bunting. Staple these onto some ribbon or tape and hang them up indoors or in your garden, Make seasonal or celebration bunting by choosing appropriate colours or drawing pictures on plain fabrics.

▶ Make 'special day' flags by drawing or painting on an old pillowcase or a rectangle of fabric and sticking this to a bamboo cane with duct tape. You could make birthday flags, festival flags, flags for parents' meetings, coffee mornings, sports days or visiting days for new children.

Links with EYFS goals

Personal, Social and Emotional Development
Social development

▶ Works as part of a group or class, taking turns and sharing fairly.

▶ Takes into account the ideas of others.

Physical Development

▶ Constructs in a purposeful way, using simple tools and techniques.

▶ Demonstrates fine motor control and coordination.

▶ Uses small and large equipment, showing a range of basic skills.

▶ Handles tools, objects, construction and malleable materials safely and with basic control.

▶ Demonstrates coordination and control in large and small movements, and in using tools and equipment.

Dolls clothes - new clothes for Barbie and Superman

Making simple clothes for favourite characters is a great way of involving children in simple sewing and sticking.

What you need

- ▶ thin, easily managed fabrics
- ▶ a range of character figures – superheroes, small dolls such as Barbie, Human TV and film characters (or suggest that children bring their own from home)
- ▶ sharp children's scissors
- ▶ needles and threads
- ▶ glue, tape, small pegs and clips
- ▶ elastic bands, string and cotton
- ▶ felt pens and decorations, such as sequins, beads, tape and glitter

What you do

1. Before you start, make sure you are offering a range of fabrics in different colours, patterns and styles. Make sure you have pastel colours, deep colours, stripes, patterns and flowers. The fabrics should be easy to cut and soft enough to drape.

2. Talk with the children about the clothes they could make for the figures you have collected. You could discuss what Superman wears when he goes to bed, what Barbie wears when it rains, whether Spiderman needs a cape etc.

3. Look together at the fabrics you have chosen, and talk about who might wear them and when.

4. Now let the children use the fabrics and other resources to make some new clothes for their figures, helping them if they need it. Children will often fashion quite complex costumes for dolls and figures, and will find ways to fix them with or without sewing, as long as you provide them with manageable fabrics and inspiring resources.

5. Encourage tearing, snipping, wrapping, and the use of glue, elastic bands and pegs. Be accepting of the methods they use, suggesting without dominating. The idea of the activity is to be creative and imaginative, not perfect!

And another idea...

▶ Photograph the costumes and accessories they make and use the photos to make a clothing catalogue for character figures.

▶ Try making clothes for bigger dolls, teddies and other soft toys.

▶ Make some beds and bedclothes for the characters, using small boxes, sheeting, soft fleece for blankets etc.

▶ Try using fabrics to line boxes and baskets for storage, for picnics and for snack resources, such as beakers and cutlery. Make a picnic basket for the role-play area.

Links with EYFS goals

Creative Development

▶ Explores different media and responds to a variety of sensory experiences.

▶ Tries to capture experiences using a variety of different media.

▶ Explores colour, texture, shape, form and space in two or three dimensions.

▶ Uses imagination in art and design.

▶ Responds in a variety of ways to what they see, hear, smell, touch and feel.

▶ Expresses and communicates ideas, thoughts and feelings using a range of materials, suitable tools, imaginative role-play, movement, designing and making, and a variety of songs and musical instruments.

▶ Expresses feelings and preferences in response to artwork, drama and music, and makes some comparisons and links between different pieces.

▶ Responds to their own work and that of others when exploring and communicating ideas, feelings and preferences through art.

Socks and mittens – little gnomes

Recycling socks and mittens is a good way to use all those odd ones that have lost their partners. This activity is not strictly sewing, but will lead nicely into some similar, but more challenging ideas.

What you need

▶ socks in any colour, but preferably plain and ideally green – children's socks are ideal

▶ rice, dried beans or lentils for filling

▶ a disposable paper or plastic cup or yogurt pot (to help with filling)

▶ sharp scissors

▶ wool

▶ elastic bands

▶ beads or 'googly' eyes

What you do

1. Cut the bottom off the plastic or paper cup and fit it into the top of the sock to make a funnel. Then fill each sock about three-quarters full of filling.

2. Now help each child to firmly tie the top of the sock closed with a piece of wool. This will be the top of the gnome's hat.

3. Now make the gnome's nose. Let each child grab a small bunch of filling and sock about halfway down the sock and help them to wind an elastic band tightly round this bunch to make the nose.

4. Glue or sew on two black or 'googly' eyes and sit your gnomes on a window-sill.

5. A little bell or decorative bobble on the end of the gnome's hat will add a bit of sparkle.

And another idea...

▶ Make perfume bags from baby socks (white or pastel colours look good for gifts). Fill them with pot-pourri and sew or tie the tops. Decorate with flowers cut from fabric, or get some little stick-on foam shapes from a craft shop.

▶ Use brown or black socks to make cats and dogs, using the same instructions as the gnome, but tying two ears in the top of the sock, and adding whiskers and a tail made from twisted wool.

▶ Make monsters or space creatures from adult patterned socks (the wilder the better!) – tying horns, ears, noses, beaks etc. Make big eyes from beads or felt and feelers from pipe cleaners.

▶ Make bugs and spiders with black pipe cleaner legs and sock bodies filled with beans. Hang from thin elastic. These make really good toys.

Links with EYFS goals

Personal, Social and Emotional Development
Dispositions and attitudes

▶ Shows an interest in classroom activities through observation or participation.

▶ Continues to be interested, motivated and excited to learn.

▶ Is confident to try new activities, initiate ideas and speak in a familiar group.

▶ Maintains attention and concentrates.

Physical Development

▶ Demonstrates fine motor control and coordination.

▶ Uses small and large equipment, showing a range of basic skills.

▶ Handles tools, objects, construction and malleable materials safely and with basic control.

Simple dressing up – make your own tabard

Making simple dressing-up clothes is really satisfying for children, and just a few simple stitches makes a real difference when they personalise them.

What you need

- ▶ pillowcases or lengths of non-fray material about twice the length of a pillowcase
- ▶ sharp children's scissors
- ▶ children's needles, wool or embroidery threads
- ▶ hessian or Binca canvas
- ▶ glue

I will need

What you do

1. Most families have spare pillowcases that they could donate for this activity.

2. Cut a slit in the narrow, closed end of each pillowcase. Make it big enough for a child's head. Now let the children try the pillowcases on – some pillowcases are bigger than others and will fit over the children's shoulders and hips without needing to open the side seams.

3. Some will be too narrow, so slit the seams so they fit comfortably.

4. Shorten the tabard if it is too long to allow free movement.

5. Now talk about the different people who might wear these dressing-up tabards:

   ▷ doctors, nurses and other health professionals

   ▷ hairdressers

   ▷ cooks and waiters

   ▷ gardeners and wildlife experts

   ▷ firemen, postmen etc.

   ▷ story characters

6. Let the children choose how they will make a badge for their character – either sewing, sticking or drawing on small squares of canvas or hessian.

7. Help them to sew the badge onto their tabard. Many children will need help with this, and you need to be both patient and tolerant of imperfections!

And another idea...

▶ Cut the corners from some pillowcases to make bonnets or hats – add ears for animals or hair for humans.

▶ Sew wings or capes to the shoulders of tabards and transform them into superhero costumes.

▶ Make some pillowcase tabards into animal costumes by painting animal patterns on them and making twisted or plaited tails. You could also add masks made from matching fabric with knotted ears, tied round the child's face or head.

Links with EYFS goals

Communication, Language and Literacy

▶ Talks activities through, reflecting on and modifying actions.

▶ Interacts with others in a variety of contexts, negotiating plans and activities, and taking turns in conversation.

▶ Talks and listens confidently and with control, consistently showing awareness of the listener by including relevant detail.

▶ Uses language to work out and clarify ideas, showing control of a range of appropriate vocabulary.

Creative Development

▶ Explores different media and responds to a variety of sensory experiences.

▶ Tries to capture experiences using a variety of different media.

▶ Explores colour, texture, shape, form and space in two or three dimensions.

▶ Uses imagination in art and design.

▶ Responds in a variety of ways to what they see, hear, smell, touch and feel.

▶ Expresses and communicates ideas, thoughts and feelings using a range of materials, suitable tools, imaginative role-play, movement, designing and making, and a variety of songs and musical instruments.

▶ Expresses feelings and preferences in response to artwork, drama and music, and makes some comparisons and links between different pieces.

▶ Responds to their own work and that of others when exploring and communicating ideas, feelings and preferences through art.

Puppets – spider puppets

Making finger puppets from gloves is an easy and rewarding way to use odd gloves by personalising them.

What you need

- gloves with fingers - adults' or children's – dark colours work best, but any would do
- circles of dark fabric about 12cm inches across
- cotton wool

- beads or 'googly' eyes
- children's needles and threads

What you do

1. Each child needs a glove for their dominant hand – if you have left gloves, you might want to offer these to left-handers or turn them inside out to make them right handed.

2. Now give each child a circle of dark fabric to make a body for their spider. Thread a needle for each child, and help them to stitch round the edge of their fabric circle – don't cut the thread off yet!

3. Now put a small ball of cotton wool in the middle of the fabric and gently pull the thread so it gathers round the cotton wool to make a soft body.

4. Help the child to sew the body onto the glove. You may have to do this for many children but be sure to ask them if they want to try, and praise them for effort if they do.

5. Try the glove on their hand to see if the body is firmly fixed. Now they will see that the fingers of the glove are the spider's legs.

6. Sew or stick two eyes on the spider – they will need to be on the child's knuckles, so they move like real ones.

7. Put on the spider and make it walk!

And another idea...

▶ Use socks to make puppets. Stuff them with screwed-up paper to keep them in shape while the child does the features. Make mouths by pushing in the toe of the sock, and add teeth if you want. Stick or sew ears, eyes, tongue and other details. Leave the stuffing in while the glue dries.

▶ Use gloves to make finger puppets in sets by:
  ▷ making a face on each finger and wearing the whole glove.
  ▷ cutting the fingers off gloves and making each one into a different puppet.

▶ Make mittens into puppets by using the thumb as a tongue or nose and bending the top of the mitten over to make a hat or hair.

Links with EYFS goals

Physical Development

▶ Constructs in a purposeful way, using simple tools and techniques.

▶ Demonstrates fine motor control and coordination.

▶ Uses small and large equipment, showing a range of basic skills.

▶ Handles tools, objects, construction and malleable materials safely and with basic control.

▶ Demonstrates coordination and control in large and small movements, and in using tools and equipment.

Creative Development

▶ Explores different media and responds to a variety of sensory experiences.

▶ Tries to capture experiences using a variety of different media.

▶ Explores colour, texture, shape, form and space in two or three dimensions.

▶ Uses imagination in art and design.

▶ Responds in a variety of ways to what they see, hear, smell, touch and feel.

Balls and beanbags
– make a simple beanbag

Here are some ideas for making simple beanbags and balls from fabrics. Some need more sewing than others!

What you need

- ▶ felt or other fabric that doesn't fray
- ▶ cotton wool
- ▶ children's needles and threads
- ▶ felt pens

What you do

1. Cut pairs of circles, squares and triangles from felt. Make them about 15cm across, so they are easy to hold, throw and catch.

2. Help the children to stitch round the edge of a pair of shapes to join them, leaving one side for a gap. Don't cut the thread!

3. Push some cotton wool in through the gap and finish sewing the bag up – children may need some help here.

4. Personalise the bag with initials, a picture or a pattern, using felt pens.

5. These beanbags are very safe for use indoors or in restricted spaces for throwing and catching practice. If you want the bags to be a bit heavier, fill them with dried beans, rice or lentils, but don't let these get wet or the seeds will start to grow!

And another idea...

▶ Here are some more ideas for making balls and beanbags:

▷ Start with a screwed-up piece of paper and wind lots of elastic bands round and round it – this will make a really bouncy ball.

▷ Turn a glove or mitten inside out, leaving the thumb/fingers inside, and fill it with rice. Sew or tie the end and you have a ball.

▷ Start with a ball of paper and wind strips of fabric round and round it, tying on new strips as you need them. Make sure you fix or stick the last end firmly or it will unwind.

▷ Fill a ziplock bag with lentils or beans. Then wind masking tape round and round it to make a firm ball.

▷ Make beanbags like juggling balls by sewing four triangles together and stuffing them.

This one isn't strictly sewing, but it makes great use of recycled materials:

▷ Make a big ball from recycled materials by screwing up plastic carriers and filling another carrier bag with them. Tie or tape the bag closed by winding masking tape or duct tape round it. This makes a great ball for outdoors, as it is waterproof.

Links with EYFS goals

Physical Development

▶ Constructs in a purposeful way, using simple tools and techniques.

▶ Demonstrates fine motor control and coordination.

▶ Uses small and large equipment, showing a range of basic skills.

▶ Handles tools, objects, construction and malleable materials safely and with basic control.

▶ Demonstrates coordination and control in large and small movements, and in using tools and equipment.

Creative Development

▶ Explores different media and responds to a variety of sensory experiences.

▶ Explores colour, texture, shape, form and space in two or three dimensions.

Fabric crayons and paints – here I am!

Simple fabric crayons are ideal for young children. They use them just like normal crayons, but need an adult to iron the image onto fabric. Fabric paints need a bit more support, as they are used directly on the fabric.

What you need

- fabric crayons
- squares of strong paper
- cotton fabric in white or pastel colours
- an iron and ironing board
- mirrors

What you do

1. It is a good idea to demonstrate this activity first so the children know that:
    - they should not do the hot bit themselves.
    - writing (such as their names) and all their pictures will come out back to front.

4. Offer fabric crayons and strong paper for their drawing, making sure that the children know they can have another go if they are not happy with their first attempt.

5. Suggest that the children might draw a picture of their own face on a piece of paper. Remind them that they can use a mirror to check the details of their appearance.

6. When the pictures are ready, let the children watch from a safe distance as you put each picture face down on a piece of cotton fabric and iron it on the back.

7. Let the paper cool down a bit so the children can reveal their own pictures by peeling off the paper.

8. Display the self-portraits together, so the children get a real sense of belonging to their group.

And another idea...

▶ Some children might like to draw members of staff to add to the portrait gallery.

▶ Experiment with some fabric pens – these are not so easy to use as you draw directly onto the fabric. Tape the fabric to strong card to stop it sliding around.

▶ Make personalised tee shirts. Ask parents to send a clean white shirt for each child. Put some card inside the tee shirt to stop the colour from bleeding to the other layer of the shirt. Let the children decide whether to decorate the front or the back (or both). They could also do a border round the bottom of their shirt, or designs on the sleeves.

▶ Use fabric crayons to liven up dressing-up clothes, curtains and other fabrics in your role-play area.

Links with EYFS goals

Personal, Social and Emotional Development

Dispositions and attitudes

▶ Shows an interest in classroom activities through observation or participation.

▶ Selects and uses activities and resources independently.

▶ Continues to be interested, motivated and excited to learn.

▶ Is confident to try new activities, initiate ideas and speak in a familiar group.

▶ Maintains attention and concentrates.

▶ Sustains involvement and perseveres, particularly when trying to solve a problem or reach a satisfactory conclusion.

Emotional development

▶ Responds to significant experiences, showing a range of feelings when appropriate (ELG).

Creative Development

▶ Explores different media and responds to a variety of sensory experiences.

▶ Tries to capture experiences using a variety of different media.

Wax resist - candle pictures

Using all those old and broken crayons is a real recycling activity - but warm wax needs very careful supervision, so you may want to stick to these simpler ideas, particularly with younger children.

What you need

- white candles
- kitchen roll or paper towels
- pale or white cotton fabric – white tee shirt fabric is good for this activity
- pieces of strong card, such as the sides of cardboard boxes
- a thin mixture of food colouring or Brusho
- masking tape

I will need

What you do

1. Cut some squares or rectangles of tough card.

2. Cut pieces of fabric to fit the cards. Stretch the fabric over the cards and secure them with tape on the edges or the back of the card.

3. Put the candles somewhere warm (such as near a radiator, or in the sun) so they are warm but not melting. This will make them easier to draw with.

4. Wrap a warm candle in paper and show the children how to make lines and patterns on the fabric. Press hard to transfer plenty of wax to the fabric. If the candle cools down, return it to the warm place and take a different one.

5. Continue to draw until the design is thickly covering the fabric. Encourage the children to look closely – it will be difficult to see the white wax on the pale fabric, so help them to feel their picture with their fingers.

6. When the design is finished, let the children brush food colouring over their picture to reveal the white patterns of wax, or you could dip the fabric in the food colouring. The dye won't stick to the wax, leaving a white pattern on the fabric. Leave to dry before removing from the card.

7. If you want to remove the wax, put the fabric between some paper towels and gently iron it until the wax melts and soaks onto the paper.

And another idea...

▶ Grate old crayons into bun tins, so the shavings for each colour are separate. Sprinkle the shavings on fabric and iron between two sheets of absorbent paper to make a waxy abstract picture.

▶ Use a microwave to melt old crayons in plastic pots. Dip brushes in the melted wax to paint pictures and patterns. This activity needs careful supervision.

▶ Drip and drizzle cooking oil onto paper. Then paint with big brushes and thin paint. The oil will protect the paper from the paint. This is a good way to make backing paper for displays.

Links with EYFS goals

Physical Development
▶ Demonstrates fine motor control and coordination.
▶ Uses small and large equipment, showing a range of basic skills.
▶ Handles tools, objects, construction and malleable materials safely and with basic control.
▶ Demonstrates coordination and control in large and small movements, and in using tools and equipment.

Creative Development
▶ Explores different media and responds to a variety of sensory experiences.
▶ Tries to capture experiences using a variety of different media.
▶ Explores colour, texture, shape, form and space in two or three dimensions.
▶ Uses imagination in art and design.

Printing on fabric – stamp it!

Using stamps and printing on fabric is another different way of using an old favourite activity that can be adapted to all ages and occasions.

What you need

▶ cotton fabric

▶ paint in shallow trays – if you line the tray with a thin piece of foam, it will work better

▶ masking tape

▶ objects for printing such as:

▷ simple screwed-up fabric bunches

▷ kitchen and household equipment, like potato mashers, sieves and cutters

▷ familiar items, such as car tyres, shoes and boots

▷ sponges cut in different shapes

▷ bricks and blocks

▷ natural objects, such as fruit, vegetables, leaves and bark

What you do

1. Cut some fabric pieces and tape each one to a piece of card for printing. This gives a pad for the printer and stops the fabric sticking.

2. Offer a wide range of objects for printing, but not so many that the children get overwhelmed.

3. Put the paint in shallow trays and let the children experiment.

4. Some children will like to do rows and repeating patterns; others will just want to be free to design their own pattern.

5. Let the printing dry before removing it from the card. Display where the details can be seen.

And another idea...

▶ Offer different sorts of printing objects on different days.

▶ Stick string patterns on wooden bricks and use these to print with.

▶ Try printing on fabric with hands and feet to make a really individual hanging for your room.

▶ Cut potatoes, parsnips, apples and even a cabbage to use for printing. Sticking a fork in each cut vegetable or fruit will make it easier to hold.

▶ Take prints from unusual objects, such as tree bark, moss, skeleton leaves or even a fish from the fishmonger.

▶ Press objects into play dough, plasticine or clay and use these for printing. Put flowers or leaves on flattened clay, cover them with paper and roll them with a rolling pin to make unusual flower printing blocks.

Links with EYFS goals

Knowledge and Understanding of the World

▶ Observes, selects and manipulates objects and materials.

▶ Investigates objects and materials by using all their senses as appropriate.

Physical Development

▶ Demonstrates fine motor control and coordination.

▶ Uses small and large equipment, showing a range of basic skills.

▶ Handles tools, objects, construction and malleable materials safely and with basic control.

Bags and decorating them – my bag

Make or buy simple cotton bags to personalise.

What you need

- some cotton bags – buy these or make your own from old sheets or tee shirts
- tape or ribbon for handles
- fabric and felt scraps
- sharp children's scissors
- felt pens
- beads, buttons, ribbons, sequins, stickers and self-stick objects
- children's needles and threads

What you do

1. If you are making your own bags, cut fabric pieces about 25cm by 50cm from cotton fabric or felt.
2. Fold the pieces in half to form a bag.
3. Help the children to thread their needles and sew the two sides of the bag. Make sure you fasten off the ends securely.
4. Make two holes at the top of each side of the bag and tie two pieces of ribbon or tape for handles. Knot the ends securely to stop them from slipping out.

5. Now offer the children the widest range possible of resources to decorate their bags – sequins, glitter, beads, fake jewels, ribbon, fabric crayons, paints, stickers, foam shapes and anything else you can find. You could search 'bargain' and craft shops, charity shops and other sources for little objects to add to the store of decorations. Old jewellery can be dismantled to provide bits for decoration, and you could put a box out for parents to donate all those spare buttons from clothing.

And another idea...

▶ For younger children, buy some fantastic little ready made fabric bags from Three Bears Playthings at www.threebearsplaythings.co.uk. Search for Collection Bags – they are £6.50 for ten bags. Sew, stick or fabric crayon the decorations.

▶ Decorate cheap fabric shopping bags with applique, felt shapes, or fabric cut with decorative scissors.

Links with EYFS goals

Personal, Social and Emotional Development

Dispositions and attitudes

▶ Shows an interest in classroom activities through observation or participation.

▶ Displays high levels of involvement in self-chosen activities.

▶ Selects and uses activities and resources independently.

▶ Continues to be interested, motivated and excited to learn.

▶ Is confident to try new activities, initiate ideas and speak in a familiar group.

▶ Maintains attention and concentrates.

▶ Sustains involvement and perseveres, particularly when trying to solve a problem or reach a satisfactory conclusion.

Physical Development

▶ Constructs in a purposeful way, using simple tools and techniques.

▶ Demonstrates fine motor control and coordination.

▶ Uses small and large equipment, showing a range of basic skills.

▶ Handles tools, objects, construction and malleable materials safely and with basic control.

▶ Demonstrates coordination and control in large and small movements, and in using tools and equipment.

Resources and contacts

Needles
Children's needles with big eyes, in plastic and metal, are available from education suppliers and on the Internet – just put 'children's sewing needles' in a search engine to find your nearest stockist.

Needle threaders
These simple devices really help children and adults with threading needles. You can get them from craft shops and sewing suppliers.

Scissors
Invest in good scissors. Fiskars make good quality scissors for adults and round-ended ones suitable for children. Left-handed scissors are a useful addition.
There are lots of training scissor designs. You may have to experiment to find ones that suit you and the children, but they are very useful for younger or less dextrous children.

Patterned scissors

Brusho (www.colourcraftltd.com)
Brusho is a concentrated, water-based colouring powder that is safe to use with children. It has a really great range of colours, particularly for cold-dying fabrics, but it does stain, so be careful when using it, and supervise carefully.

Food colouring
You can get food colouring in big bottles from TTS at www.tts-group.co.uk.

Binca
This open weave strong canvas is available from craft shops and education suppliers.

Felt
Felt is also available from hundreds of suppliers and craft shops. Choose the one where you get best value and the widest colour range.

Plastic canvas
This is a really useful resource for free sewing as it lasts forever and can be used independently by very young children. The disadvantage is having to unpick the stitching to reuse it!

Sewing cards
Buying sewing cards is a quick way to tool up for sewing. They are easy to find on the Internet, and may inspire you to make some of your own.

Single hole punches
These are useful for punching holes in thick card or leather – you can get ones with a single hole and others with multiple holes.

Boxes and storage
Old fashioned boxes are fascinating to young children! www. sewessential.co.uk has a selection of sewing boxes and baskets